SUBURBAN POEMS

Ken Dowen

American Editions

North American Editions

KEN DOWEN

To Deb, who else.

© 1986-2020 Ken Dowen

THIRD EDITION

ISBN-978-1-7349897-9-3

All rights reserved.

No part of this book may be reproduced
or transmitted in any form or by any means,
electronic or mechanical including photo-
copying, recording, or by anyinformation
storage and retrieval system, without permis-
sion in writing from the publisher.
ken42r@yahoo.com

Design notes: included in this edition, on the
cover and within are abstract designs from the original
1986 2nd edition, *Suburban Poems* chapbook.

Contents

Look A likes   6
Congo Church   7
Remember   8
Eulogy   12
Formerly Westborough   13
Philosophers   14
Hypes of a Modern Poet   15
Utopia   17
Maybe   18
Middle Class Kitsch   19
Excuses   20
Fragments   22
New Hampshire Trip 75'   23

Preface

Suburban Poems are autobiographical poems covering the mid-sixties, the Vietnam era, and on through the eighties. All of these poems are in some ways sarcastic, satirical, ironic and naive. For some, senseless childhood "wars" in the apple orchard morphed into the senseless reality of the War in Vietnam. For this poet, the experience was part of the journey. "Look-a-likes" is about the author and his boyhood friend, Earl, "We were enemies for senseless reasons...flicking those mushy, brown and hard green apples off each others heads." And in just a few short years...

"The green skins of our sour youth turned rot red, ripe and blue..." and we, "...joined the army together under the delusion we'd both out grown something."

Other poems are Congo Church, Formerly Westborough, Hypes Of A Modern Poet, Philosophers, Remember, Utopia and Eulogy.

New to this edition; Fragments, Maybe, Excuses, Middle Class Kitsch and New Hampshire Trip 1975.

LOOK A LIKES

When Earl and I were boys
we were enemies
for senseless reasons
Flicking those
mushy, brown and
hard green apples
off each others heads...
We were 'never allies
even during supper time
cease fires.
Then, someone picked the orchard
clean of apples and trees
planted tract houses
And, the green skins
of our sour youth
turned rot red, ripe and blue.
Earl and I became friends
and joined the army together
under the delusion
we'd both outgrown something.

CONGO CHURCH

Reverend Wilson stepped down
out of the frame
his skin matte crackled
like the old oil painting
where he lived
in a room
off the chapel
Globs of silver hair
shoot out the side of his head
over the tips of his pale pink ears
He shook my kid sticky hand
I felt the chock dust
of white church clapboards
on the tips of my fingers.

REMEMBER?

Remember me
running faster
than my nose
home from school,
first grade
Teacher walked us to the library,
I was so excited
We held hands along the way
So smooth and sticky...
Can't you see her?
We didn't live up
to your expectations
Couldn't accept
your explanations...
She is my generation
she grew beside me, in me, by me,
rode me, rocked me, sat astride me
Grew our hair together,
see sawed
teeter totter, unique obliques
finding energy
found guilty...
abusing freedom-
Remember?
Remember the search we did for the soul-
Karma, Christ, Buddhas of Gold?
Some of us found, some of us stole,
Those of us left, left out in the cold,

Where we...
wave our empty heads and hands
and strain to see molecules
without microscopes.

Where we make holes in concrete
with the tips of our fingers,
Where we plead for peace ...
with a whisper of flowers
and Vietnam meadows linger...
Where we write poems
on steamed-up glass.
Remember?
"What are you on?" You said
So we bury our losses
in nap sacks, in back packs
in dungaree pockets
Where the weight
anchors us to the ground.

Remember

    "What are you on?"

You said.
So we bury our losses
in nap sacks n' back packs
n' dungaree pockets
Where the weight
anchors us to the ground.

EULOGY

Dylan Thomas swallowed one last glob
of New York air and disappeared into
who know where? And the buses ran
on schedule...
Jack Benny croaked after one last joke
and the boob tube pitched Brillo pads
into the brittle brain of A harried
Jersey housewife as her husband reached
for a day old hunk of rye toast
And the buses ran on schedule.
Kennedy died
and his name became known
in the only village in the world
where they didn't already know
and so many thousands cried
and so many thousands
kept appointments
And the buses ran on schedule.
Jack, my friend was sucked
through his trumpet
in the heat of his young breath
one spring afternoon
And my watch ticked on
And the buses ran on schedule.

KEN DOWEN

FORMERLY WESTBOROUGH

For the sake of progress,
They took the "UGH" out of Westboro
They took the "UGH" out of Westboro
to be contemporary...
They took the "UGH" out of Westboro
to economize, cheaper highway signs
They took the "UGH"out of Westboro
to attract industry and shopping malls
But now the "UGH"
back in Westborough
Westborough is progressive...

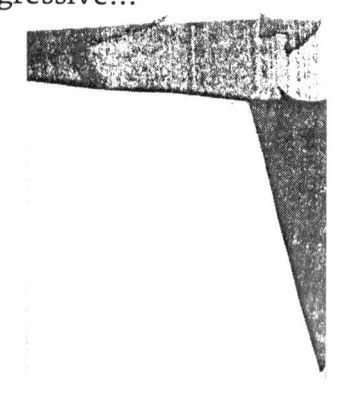

Ugh!

PHILOSOPHERS

"Man.... This is it....Man!"
"So this is what ever'body been talkin' bout
for so long, huh?"
"You eve' hear of Nostradamus, Man?"
"'No stra....who? Man"
"Aw never mine. Dylan said it too, Man.
You know, 'blowin' in the wind'".
"Which Dylan was that, Man?"
"I don' know. Hey! Check it out!
Look-e those dudes runnin' round—
Mass hysteria, Man!"
"Yeah! Well, where's that God everybody
gives their bread too? Yeah! Where is that dude
all the monks used to rap on n' on 'bout?"
"I don 'know, Bro". You got any Reefer? Hey, is it getting dark?"
"Damn right! I get scared, Man."
"Aw! Is natural t'b scarred in the dark, Man....
"I guess you right, the sun 'ill rise t'morrow."
"You know that dog of mine, Man,
knows no fear!"
"Your dog is cool--really cool, Man."

KEN DOWEN

HYPES OF A MODERN POET

It's two A.M.
I sit naked, staring at impatient
poetic tools lying dormant
at the tips of my fingers
mayhem erupts; the world still absurd
is impaled on my pen
inspired by self-satisfaction
Each word is born of reluctance, fear
science and God-heads dictate my function
by gnawing at my flesh, tearing at my nostril
ignoring my manhood.
The blank screen reflects the light of my writing lamp
My eyes become fixed on the cold, gray glass
parent to my children, administrator of information,
gateway to conformity...
The double-pawed cat, black and white, I envy
as it pities me and my race wars, cities, fires,
inflation's, politicians, murders, furniture sales, special offers.

As if it knew of brotherhood, hate, suicide,
Moonies, music, moods and nature.
As if it knew love,
As if it knew of men
not doomed as shallow figures
Who's shadows shout static
from the darkness decaying
in the horizontal skull of concrete
glass and steel

Wordsworth lies on a cool slab
in a cold house.
Among the androids,

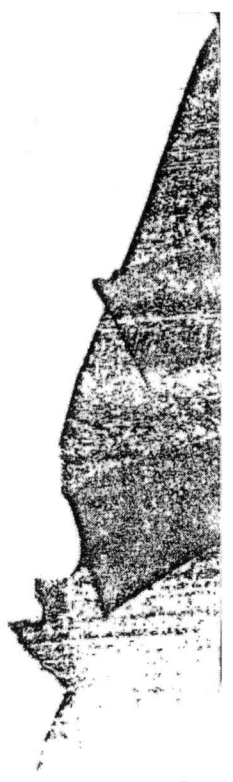

several frustrated poets
express their individuality
and realize the
ominous age of the
computer poem anthology.

UTOPIA?

I'm just searching for survival
Doing a 'Hustle' and a 'Disco dancin'
I see kids camped on suitcases
by the side of the road
and curled up on a father's chest
I see the mother—thumb out-- hitching a ride
Fast..., the super cars pass
leaving clouds of clinging dust
in the cool Autumn air
UTOPIA?
I'm just toasting my feet in the
electric heat and couldn't care less about
who, is melting now in the snow,
who, is to be buried by
Eighteen point bucks of business
who fly with attack eagles,
who's clinging claws clutch
their massive shoulders
who defecate—white feces falling in creamy
earth bound droplets.
It's all so melodramatic.

MAYBE

Maybe,
If I think of a friend...
Some light flashes of past...
Sniffing grass, pumping gas,
cold ocean climbing my skin
my child's sweet tears
no earth dam could contain
and those soft love refrains
I could write just one more poem.

Waldon Pond, Concord, Massachusetts
    Photo by the author

MIDDLE CLASS KITSCH

In the mono sodium glutamate
covered city
the masses ogled
synthetic black velvet paintings
of Christ, elves and horny unicorns
Wishing to hang one or all behind
a leopard skin divan
they thrust deeply
into polyester pockets
without ever feeling a thing...
into the cool dark between trinket receipts...
and grocery store checkout slips...
into the moist vacuum where money hangs out
and before they knew it,
they were calling themselves
patrons of the arts.

EXCUSES

We waited for the train
sat in the family wagons
aside of each other -buddies
nervous -buddies
I had to piss
would have,
on the wheels of the car
one of those situations
there was nothing else in '67
nothing except to get the fuck
out of the house
nothing except to get the fuck
out of town
The train,
bellied us in
to Boston
to the Navy base
to join some emancipating Army
to become man
to learn shooting sperm
into a New Jersey party girl
to become man
to yell" kill!"
to become man
to push up, out, in, down
on command
to" pull our heads up out of our asses"
to respect the starch on someone's fatigues
who claims to be
everyone's mother, father, sister, brother.
Brother?
to bivouac, march and love leadership...
to U.S.A.R.V

to become a men...
men without hair...
the Butcher barber...
sweeps it into the garbage heap
with the rest of our independence...
to the hot, landscape of Asia
to become man...
to awaken in the morning light...
to look out upon the
organically barren
barrack strewn landscape...

Where pointed hats
on small dark heads
bob up and down
on the way
to everyday monotony
Two boys barely twelve
eyes fixed straight ahead
with heavy shoulder loads
walking bent over like old soldiers
because there was
nothing else to do!

FRAGMENTS

...scattered about the landscape
by winds and exhaled breaths
a piece of me here and there
gradually... I disappear!
Carried off by insects
and sudden gusts
Gather only what you need...
that father's arm
or lover's tongue
that leering eyeball or two
                      leave the rest
                      I'm fragments
                      nothing whole anymore
                      and I'm everywhere.

NEW HAMPSHIRE TRIP 1975

The mountains off the highway right and left
blasting color with sun in my eyes
miles flashing on the odometer
as rapid as the guardrail polls
farm houses and barns
and pastures going by,
not as rapid
smoking grass and looking for
a State package store.
Small cabin, four friends, burning logs
goin' to the Pike general store
to buy some beer and shingles tacks
drinking on the ride to Moosilauke
to drink some more and unwind
drunk until sick enough
to promise self prohibition
climbing black mountain
with four-wheel drive
different poets, different mountain
walking up in endless hard terrain.

To the top
climbing a former fire lookout station
broken glass, fifty mile winds,
compass view in all directions,
flying a kite from the top
loose string,

slips away from my shaking fingers
off the craggy mountain
into the trees
getting high twice
and getting higher still at the top
until it's time to go down
for endless stories about the trip
to tell at times
when fires and remembrance are burning...
when the traps are decorated
with small animals
and snow is deep all around
and your ass is numb
sitting on the wooden plank
in the crude outhouse.

American Editions

Made in the USA
Monee, IL
03 June 2020